First Facts™

Exploring the Animal Kingdom

Fish

goatfish

by Adele Richardson

Consultant:
Robert T. Mason
Professor of Zoology, J. C. Braly Curator of Vertebrates
Oregon State University
Corvallis, Oregon

Capstone
press

Mankato, Minnesota

First Facts is published by Capstone Press
151 Good Counsel Drive, P.O. Box 669, Mankato, Minnesota 56002
www.capstonepress.com

Library of Congress Cataloging-in-Publication Data
Richardson, Adele, 1966–
    Fish / by Adele Richardson.
        p. cm.—(First facts. Exploring the animal kingdom)
    Includes bibliographical references and index.
    ISBN 0-7368-2622-X (hardcover)
    1. Fishes—Juvenile literature. I. Title. II. Series.
QL617.2.R528 2005
597—dc22   2004000667

Summary: Discusses the characteristics, eating habits, and offspring of fish,
    one of the main groups in the animal kingdom.

Editorial credits
Erika L. Shores, editor; Linda Clavel, designer; Kelly Garvin, photo researcher;
    Eric Kudalis, product planning editor

Photo credits
Bruce Coleman Inc./Jane Burton, 17; Phil Degginger, 9; Tim O'Keefe, 20
Capstone Press/Gary Sundermeyer, cover (top left)
Corbis/John Madere, 16; Marty Snyderman, cover (middle left)
Creatas, cover (main right)
Digital Vision/Stephen Frink, 11, 15
Eda Rogers, 18
Photodisc Inc., 1, 6–7, 12–13; G. K. & Vikki Hart, cover (bottom left)
Seapics.com/Doug Perrine, 19; James D. Watt, 10

Table of Contents

Fish 4

Fish Are Vertebrates 6

Fish Are Cold-Blooded 8

Bodies of Fish 10

Fish Have Scales 13

How Fish Breathe 14

What Fish Eat 16

Eggs and Young 18

Amazing but True! 20
Compare the Main Animal Groups 21
Glossary 22
Read More 23
Internet Sites 23
Index 24

Fish

Fish belong to the animal kingdom. Stingrays, sharks, and goldfish are fish.

Five other main groups of animals live on earth with fish. Birds have feathers. Reptiles have hard, dry skin. Amphibians have moist skin. Insects have three body sections and six legs. Mammals have hair.

Birds

Mammals

Reptiles

Main Animal Groups

Insects

Amphibians

Fish

Fish Are Vertebrates

Fish have backbones. Animals with backbones are **vertebrates**. A fish's **skeleton** is joined to its backbone. Some fish have skeletons made of bone.

Rays and sharks are fish that have skeletons made of **cartilage**. Cartilage is a strong tissue that bends more than bone does.

blue-spotted stingray

Fish Are Cold-Blooded

Fish are cold-blooded animals. Their body temperatures change with the water around them. Fish swim to a new area when the water temperature changes. During summer, a bass lives near the warm surface of a lake. In winter, the bottom of the lake is warmer. The bass swims to the bottom then.

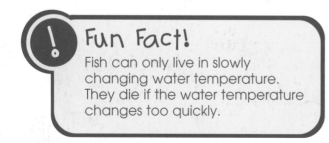

Fun Fact!
Fish can only live in slowly changing water temperature. They die if the water temperature changes too quickly.

largemouth bass

Bodies of Fish

All fish have a body, a head, and a tail. Tuna have torpedo-shaped bodies. This long, narrow shape helps them swim quickly through water.

yellowfin tuna

Fish have **fins**. Fins help a fish move through the water. Angelfish use their fins to swim between rocks.

blue chromis

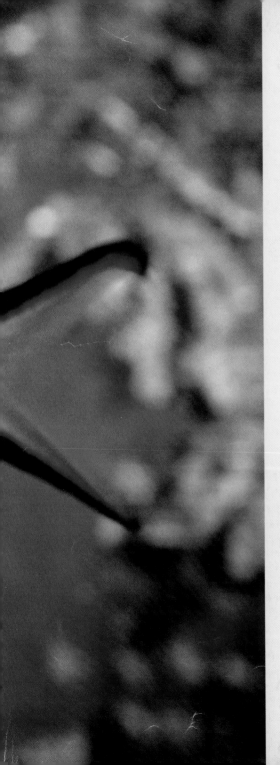

Fish Have Scales

This blue chromis and most other fish have skin covered with **scales**. Some fish have scales that are smooth. Other fish have rough scales that look like tiny teeth. Scales help protect fish from **predators**.

! Fun Fact!
Some kinds of freshwater catfish and eels do not have scales.

How Fish Breathe

Sharks and other fish breathe in water. Water moves through a fish's mouth and over its **gills**. The gills take **oxygen** from the water. The oxygen then enters the fish's blood. Animals need oxygen in their blood to live.

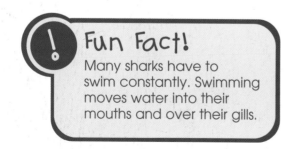

Fun Fact!
Many sharks have to swim constantly. Swimming moves water into their mouths and over their gills.

red-bellied piranha

What Fish Eat

Fish eat many kinds of food. Most fish eat other animals. This piranha catches fish with its sharp teeth.

Some fish eat plants. Goldfish eat plants in a pond. Other fish eat plants growing on rocks.

Eggs and Young

Most fish **hatch** from eggs. Female
fish usually lay many eggs at one
time. Other fish eat many of the eggs
before they can hatch.

Some fish, like sharks, give birth to live young. The young grow inside a female's body until they are born.

lemon sharks

Amazing but True!

Walking catfish can move on land. The fish digs its fins into the ground. Its body wriggles like a snake to move forward. The walking catfish has organs that help it breathe air. The fish can live for several days out of water.

Compare the Main Animal Groups

	Vertebrates	Invertebrates	Warm-blooded	Cold-blooded	Hair	Feathers	Scales
Fish	X			X			X
Amphibians	X			X			
Birds	X		X			X	
Insects		X		X			
Mammals	X		X		X		
Reptiles	X			X			X

Glossary

cartilage (KAR-tuh-lij)—the strong, rubbery body tissue that makes up the skeletons of some fish

fin (FIN)—a body part of a fish that is shaped like a flap

gill (GIL)—a body part on the side of a fish that helps it get oxygen from water

hatch (HACH)—to break out of an egg

oxygen (OK-suh-juhn)—a colorless gas in the air or water that animals need to breathe

predator (PRED-uh-tur)—an animal that hunts other animals for food

scales (SKALES)—small, hard pieces of skin that cover the bodies of most fish

skeleton (SKEL-uh-tuhn)—the bones or cartilage that support and protect the body

vertebrate (VUR-tuh-bruht)—an animal that has a backbone

Read More

Harvey, Bev. *Fish.* Animal Kingdom. Philadelphia: Chelsea Clubhouse Books, 2003.

Heinrichs, Ann. *Fish.* Nature's Friends. Minneapolis: Compass Point Books, 2003.

Sill, Cathryn P. *About Fish: A Guide for Children.* Atlanta: Peachtree Publishers, 2002.

Internet Sites

FactHound offers a safe, fun way to find Internet sites related to this book. All of the sites on FactHound have been researched by our staff.

Here's how:
1. Visit *www.facthound.com*
2. Type in this special code **073682622X** for age-appropriate sites. Or enter a search word related to this book for a more general search.
3. Click on the **Fetch It** button.

FactHound will fetch the best sites for you!

Index

angelfish, 11

backbones, 6
bass, 8
blue chromis, 13
breathing, 14

cartilage, 6
catfish, 13
cold-blooded, 8

eels, 13
eggs, 18

fins, 11, 20
food, 16–17

gills, 14
goldfish, 4, 17

oxygen, 14

piranha, 16
predators, 13

rays, 4, 6

scales, 13
sharks, 4, 6, 14, 19
skeletons, 6

tails, 10
tuna, 10

vertebrates, 6

walking catfish, 20
water, 8, 10, 11, 14, 20